Mechanical Bell Sunrises

A book of poems
by
Diane Lincoln

First Printing: 2020

ISBN 0-9744254-0-0

Diane M. Lincoln
Geneva, IL

dianelincoln01@gmail.com

Special discounts are available to educators and on quantity purchases. For details, contact the publisher at the above-listed address.

To my family for their continued support
through all the craziness.

Table of Contents

Acknowledgements

I would like to thank my teachers for instilling in me the love for writing, Poetry SIG members (too many to name) for sharing their knowledge, the Early Risers for their comradery, Virginia Kammerer's group for their editing suggestions, Roberta Stewart and John Buckley for introducing me to *Arts Beat,* and Open Sky Poets for providing the cookies that helped to reinspire me. And, special thanks to my husband, Don Lincoln, for his unyielding patience and assistance with the cover art and with all aspects of the blasted technology. Without any one of these people, this book would never have been completed.

Preface

Thank you so much for your interest in my poetry. Writing has been a love of mine for many years. I am delighted to be able to share my work with you.

I have arranged this book into four parts. "Modern Life" poems were inspired by our artificial world. Politics, el trains, and the stress of dealing with the world are topics you will find there. "Art and Musings" are poems about the arts, writing, and the craft of poetry. "A Female Perspective" includes some romantic poems, but there are also some that express my own unique perspective. Poems about family, aging and the dynamics brought about by the human condition can be found under the title, "Consequences of Birth."

Please do not trust any of the content of these writings to be autobiographical. For instance, I was not in high school in 1968, Tom never cheated, and *Coffee* was inspired by the loss of Peggy.

As I send this to the printer, my only regret is that my dear friend, Frank Rutledge, never saw this collection come to fruition.

I sincerely hope that all who read this will be happy they did.

MODERN LIFE

A View of the Cage

Our derelict building had staircases
with distressed wooden railings,
Z-shapes, one on top of another
making an elaborate cage.

An unusable area
allotted to teens
was the dirty, flat roof of a brick garage
between the building
and the el trains.

There, in the grit
and the heavy smell of hot metal,
we drank pilfered beer
smoked a variety of flavors
hung out for hours, weeks, lifetimes.

When forced to freeze,
interrupted by a passing train,
we watched reflected
blue sparks of the el
scream along our cage.

In the silence of each din,
You could reflect
If you dared.

When I Quit Smoking

I didn't change;
The world did.
Buses always take longer now,
the food in diners never tastes good,
coffee needs cream & sugar,
and more people have bad breath.
But the worst is that it's impossible
to strike up a conversation.

The Granite State

In New Hampshire you could see
A rock formation, a great stone face
Affectionately known as
The Old Man of the Mountain

The Granite State is also the place
Where hopefuls vie
For candidacy

About the "Old Man," Daniel Webster once said,
"Just as a shoemaker hangs out a shoe,
God put the Old Man there to show the world
That New Hampshire is where men are made."

New Hampshire's primaries gave us
Men like Roosevelt, Eisenhower, and Kennedy
Under the watchful eye
Of the Old Man of the Mountain

A short time ago that beloved old man
Fell in a thunder from the mountainside.
The New Hampshire primaries will continue to make men
But from today's shameless, money-driven, quests,
It appears that God has withdrawn his endorsement.

* "The Granite State" was previously published in the *Kane County Chronicle*.

Hearts and Flowers

Hearts and flowers all in a row
Horrors and heartbreaks ahead.
Copy from the glossary.
Fill in the blanks.
Behave as if
The ozone protects you,
The air is not growing thick,
The oceans are not
Filling with greed.
Study your lessons
As if tomorrow were yesterday.
Hearts and flowers all in a row.

Tinsel

There's something about tinsel on a tree.
You can keep all the flashy, blinky stuff.
Give me the subtle movements
Of sparkles dancing,
Reflecting more than light.
Memories twinkle in the tinsel
A grandmother's house,
The scent of pine and baked goods,
And the taste of cocoa.

Sometimes It's Hard to Live in the Moment

Got up early
Got the kids bathed, fed and dressed
Myself too
Hair combed, last minute adjustments
Sped the loaded car.
Finally, all lined-up in the pew
Shh, shh, it's the story about the fishes
Fish, that's a good idea
Can wrap it in aluminum foil
We have the necessary spices
White wine, open, in the back of the fridge
But what else? Rice?
No. I have to remember to put that
(and, oh yeah, shampoo) on the list
Potatoes? No
Loaves of bread! That's it!
But do we have butter?

* "Sometimes It's Hard to Live in the Moment" was previously published in *Nanny Fanny Magazine* and *The Chaffin Journal*. This poem also won a Poets and Patrons Awards Honorable Mention in the category of Humorous Verse.

It Occured to Me

You mow your grass, cut the hedges
And trim along the sidewalk's edges.
While I'm on the pavement, my feet igniting,
Your lawn is looking so inviting

I thought how wonderful it would be
To cut across your soft, cool green.

That's when it occurred to me,
That grass was made to be walked on
And not conformed into a lawn.

* "It Occurs to Me" and "Mechanical Bell Sunrises" were the first
  poems I wrote (with the exception of the one about the Easter
  Bunny that I penned in second grade).

A Tainted Feather

The Archangel
fought with God
falling from heights
at vision-blurred speed
barely slowed by Earth.
A tainted feather or two
loosened from his wings as he fell
leaving behind evil,
that poisoned the world.

If we accept that story,
we could believe
that war and hate
are not our fault.

The Grown Little Girl

Gray haired and accomplished
she harbors a hurt.
The grown little girl,
who walked past the guards
as her mother instructed,
breathes remembering the unliving.
Decades of safety can fade
at the sound of
a Polish word spoken
or the horrible, heavy
rumble of a train.
Even a sunny day
can bring memories
of hiding
longing for parents
who would never return.
Surviving is not enough
to heal the pain.

* "The Grown Little Girl" was my friend and fellow poet, Helen
   Degen Cohen, who died at the age of 81 in November, 2015.
   I like to think that she has been reunited with her loved ones.

Signs of Spring

The old white farmhouse stood back from the road
Its drive was flanked by two huge oaks.
Often this scene held a sign
Announcing a completion or a beginning.

"Strawberries" the hand-painted sign said
When the trees showed their patchwork of country colors.
And when the trees became a display of
Black lace against a white sky,
The sign read, "Home Made Gifts."

The changing of the guard outside that farmhouse
Became an indicator for me
Predicting the coming season while tenderly closing the last.

One spring when their giant arms were spread wide
In a celebration of water and sparkling shades of green,
A sign cut in the shape of a sewing machine
Announced, "Antiques for Sale."

Then, that summer when the "Firewood" sign appeared
The look-alikes were clad in such heavy, dark green quilts,
I thought it was their fullness
That made the house and other trees invisible from the road.

It wasn't until later that the barren truth was revealed to me.
A gravel drive overtaken by weeds, leading to emptiness
Two stumps were all that remained of those beloved trees.
Then, only then, did I recall the signs
That forecasted the season I had not foretold.

Years later, every time I pass that place
I'm haunted by a pair of tall, twin ghosts
And an old white farmhouse that stood back from the road.

Life Goes On

It's about the plague
The stench of death
And bodies

But he doesn't know that
He just likes the
"all fall down" part

I watch and smile
As he shouts it,
Bounces, and giggles

I Hear Geneva

You sing to me
My city on the Fox.
A retreat from Broad Shoulders
Your quaint charm calls to me.

Among the trains and bridges
I hear the mystic chant
Of the native tribe at Big Spring
Celebrating prosperity held herein.

From the shadow of the courthouse
Seven score years later
I still hear young men clamoring
For news and for glory.

History whispers
Of mills, glucose, and creameries.
A city built of logs and river stone
Forged a time yet untold.

Among antiques and boutiques
Wainscoting and bay windows
A present-day haven
In a sparkling valley of lights
Geneva calls to me ...
Välkommen.

* "I Hear Geneva" was previously published in *The Kane County Chronicle* and it was featured in *Art Around the Fox.*

When the Snowflakes Come Down

My favorite day of the year
is when the snowflakes come down.
At the first sign of snow,
we drink cocoa and sing songs.
We gather at the table and cut out
cute paper snowflakes to decorate windows.

Then one day, at the end of a blizzardous commute,
after surviving countless hazards,
with cold fingers and toes,
I arrive home,
park, climb over the plow heap,
and trudge through what appears to be
an endless white driveway.
That's when my eye catches the cute paper flakes
and I remember the fun we had
back when we made them.

Nonetheless, that glorious Spring day
when those snowflakes finally come down
is my favorite day of the year.

Sad and Helpless

As the names were spoken
The church bells marked the time
Names read from the quilt
One name at a time

While every quarter hour
The bells chimed in the tower
The names kept being read
One after another

The church bells told
Of funeral bells
Each name a silenced voice
And yet the bells continued
Every quarter hour
Hour after hour

Arboretum Sonnet

I signed-up for the arboretum class
Because I was so taken by the trees.
The notion was that I could fondly pass
The hours reading underneath their leaves.
I'd watch the maple branches change their hue
As willow fingers gently brush the Earth
Then seek out where the largest oak tree grew
And walk around to marvel at its girth.
But I had been the victim of a joke.
It wasn't long before I figured out
That *Quercus Alba* is the mighty oak
And Latin was what this was all about.
    I'm sure that science cares about a tree
    But love is left for poets, you and me.

We Keep Looking

Beyond the
  background noise
Before
  quarks
  and heat
When all the laws
  did not exist
Before the time of time
Is that where we will find You?

High School 1968

I don't recall what we talked about
That afternoon sitting by the window
In the restaurant near school

But I remember afterwards
How you winced as I tweezed pieces
Of glass from your face

Someone had nominated a black girl
For homecoming queen

The Bandwagon

I parked my car just in time
To see a group of geese
Strutting across the empty street.

They moved as one.
All eyes fixed straight ahead
Like policemen in riot-control stance.
With pride-inflated chests
They advanced
Together
Deliberate
Focused

I scanned the horizon
To see what was going on.
Then I realized
They were geese.

Mechanical Bell Sunrises

In an era of mechanical bell sunrises
And colors of stop and go
What is real and what is not
Is sometimes hard to know.

Where brilliant artificial lights
Upon the street are flashed
The moon is not a factor
In where your shadow's cast.

Where Mother Nature's kept in check
Within a concrete shell
What is real and what is not
Is often hard to tell.

* "Mechanical Bell Sunrises" was one of the first poems I wrote.
  It was previously published in *Elmhurst Imprints*, and it was the
  poem for which the Carl H. Carlson Award for Creative Writing
  was bestowed.

File This One Under: Just in Case You Care

Niccoli Cabibbo,
in 1963
said the strong and weak forces
treat mesons differently

Those Little Pigs

I never liked those little pigs
Who took advantage of their brother's digs
They shoddily worked, never caring a lick
While he toiled away with mortar and brick

If the brother's efforts had been combined
The resulting home could've been divine
An open floor plan, central heating and air
Three bedrooms and baths with rooms to spare

Once they had finished this ideal space
Is when their happy frolicking could take place

Esperanto*

Ci tiuj vortoj
Estas la restaĵoj,
La fantomo de lingo
Intencita por savi mondo,
Lingvo, kia reniam
Renkontis sian potencialon.
Morta sen vivi.

Ci tiuj vortoj
Sendi ilia averto al nin ne suferi
La sama destino.

English Translation:

These words
Are what remains,
The ghost of a language
Meant to save the world,
A language that never
Met its potential.
Dead without living.

These words
Warn us not to suffer
The same fate.

* Esperanto is a language, invented in 1887, meant for
  international use. "Esperanto" translates into English as "one
  who hopes."

First Year Chemistry

H_2O doesn't have two O's.
They say it's easy once you know how it goes.
But I thought first year chemistry
Was going to be the death of me.

I still haven't figured out why
Chemists put the negative ions
On the right-hand side
Instead of on the left like a number line.

And what about this measure they call pH?
It's the only scale I know that goes up to the base.
Sulfate and phosphate have four O's, not eight.
And there is no two in bi-carbonate!
If that's not enough to make you confused,
The atom that gains is called reduced.

Just for the record, so everyone knows,
2HO would have two O's.

* "First Year Chemistry" was previously published in *The Kane County Chronicle Neighbors Section.*

Energy Cycle

the fire of the sun
warms us;
through plants
it feeds us.
in the earth
remains of ancient plants
that absorbed the sun
heat our homes
run our cars.
the fire of the sun
drives the wind
nourishes our bodies
keeps everything moving
and sometimes
through us
creates poetry.

Horses

I pay bills,
Keep the house clean,
Shop, do laundry, and
Obey traffic laws.
But there are horses inside me.

Some are noble, elegant horses
Majestic in appearance
Courageous and proud
They stand ready to fight injustice

Some are graceful, wonderous creatures
Related to unicorns and to Pegasus
They are inexplicable
Vaulting with imagination

Some are impetuous, untamed, sensuous beasts
Keen, vivacious and impulsive
They rail against restraints
They are the feisty, cowboy-bucking type

I pay bills,
Keep the house clean,
Shop, do laundry, and
Obey traffic laws.
But there are horses inside me.

The End of Democracy

Oh say can you see by the dawn's early light

> Ben Franklin said:
> we would have a republic
> only if we could keep it.

What so proudly we hailed at the twilight's last gleaming

> Jefferson explained:
> only an educated populous
> can maintain a democracy.

Oh say, does that star-spangled banner yet wave

> Justice Souter warned us:
> if we do not educate ourselves
> someone will step up and offer
> to solve all of our problems and,
> that would be the end of democracy

O'er the land of the free and the home of the brave.

Only the Wind

The blanket of Venus
Was too heavy for her sister

Charts rose but too few voices stirred;
Only the wind revealed a temper

The first to go were buried with tears
Those remaining
Were left uncovered
When all the forests fell silent

Candles

Candles near the entrance
prompt thoughts of heaven.
Stories of stained-glass saints
cast a magical hue.
Incense bathes the imposing space
with an ancient perfume.

The stage was set for a white-robed man
to sing of timeless mysteries.

But there are no candles anymore.
Lust spreads a dreadful stain.
The priest's robes leave him exposed;
his groin as hungry as any man's.

Never Again

I had a roommate once
It was kinda' fun
She showed me how
To cook some meals
And cut my hair myself

Then one night
Naked
She came into my room
Put eyelashes on her breasts
And tried to climb my closet shelf

So Much for That Idea

They suggest quieting your head
By looking out the window
But lots of little bird tops
Elusive as memories
Bob up and down in the grass.
Squirrels of thought leap
Through branches of fact and fancy.
A bunny under the fence
Is unable to decide on a side.
And you just know there are
Crawly bugs of doubt
Everywhere.

Depressed

I go from focusing
on how broken the world is
to being sickeningly
sentimental about the past.
Then, on really bad days,
I realize that the past
wasn't so great either.

ART AND MUSINGS

Monet's Haystacks

It's funny how different things look
When the lighting is changed
Like how the slow playing sax
On a summer day
Sounds mellow and relaxing.
But on a rainy evening
That same slow sax
Has a melancholy feeling.

* "Monet's Haystacks" was previously published in *Arts Beat*

The Field Trip Picture

You know the one.
The teacher told us
To pay attention to technique
Look closely at how the little dots
Make up the scene.

When the class stopped to look at it
I didn't care about the dots.
I thought about how the picnic
Could be right here
On the grassy shore
Of Lake Michigan

If not for this building full of pictures.

* "The Field Trip Picture" was previously published in *Batavia Library Writers' 11th Literary Annual.* The art mentioned is: *A Sunday Afternoon on the Island of LaGrande Jatte,* by Georges Seurat. And, just for the record, now that I'm grown-up, I love the painting and the Art Institute of Chicago.

Dandelions

Bright yellow on green
Vivid
The way some people see the past
A myriad of toddler's bouquets
A crown from a bygone day

I prefer
The tall, unpredictable poofs
Ready to release the future
Into the wind

* "Dandelions" was previously published in *Bellowing Ark*.

Cultures: A Pirouette* Poem

Aseptic procedures
Are practiced in the lab.
Care must be taken where
Within a plastic tray
    conflicting cultures loom.
    Conflicting cultures loom:
A mosque, a synagogue,
An ancient Latin mass.
Philosophies abound
Upon an orb of blue.

* A Pirouette is a 10-line poem with 6 syllables per line. Lines 5 and 6 repeat with a different meaning, creating the turn around.

Make Believe

Once upon a time
(That's how you know it's not true)
There was a beautiful princess.
She lived in a grand castle;
And was doted on by a handsome prince.
The weather was always nice,
And laughter filled the air,
But, alas, the princess was not happy.
(That's how you know,
given the way the world treats women,
it really could be true)

Listening

As I lie awake listening
It begins as no more than a rumble
Far off in the distance.
Then an ever-quickening patter
    A splashing basketball game
    My reflective patrol belt
    Galoshes with elastic buttons
    Thunder
    Lightning
    Gray sky
    Dots in a puddle
Listening, I am swallowed by the rain

Muse

She sits patiently
Playing with an idea
Waiting for me
She sings silently

While I'm stuck
In the mud
Of grocery lists and
Schedules

Aware that she waits
Perfecting something beautiful
I must attend to her
Lest she fall asleep
And lose the tune

My First Shakespearean

I've never tried my muse this way before
(A sonnet in the style of The Bard).
To write ten beat per line, no less or more
While rhyming every other line, is hard.
So as you read, don't be too tough on me.
Enjoy the effort I have made instead.
I'm using all my creativity
For rhyme I have to plan two lines ahead.
And yet my greatest challenge seems to be
In adding proper meter to the mix.
The need to tap my fingers constantly
Goes well beyond my normal bag of tricks.
    Alas, dear reader, now that it's all done,
    I must confess, it was a lot of fun.

* "My First Shakespearean" appeared in the *Batavia Library Writers' 10th Literary Annual.*

Hokusai's Message

Claw-like waves tear the shore
Yet Mt. Fuji towers.
Yin and Yang maintain balance,
Hold each other in place,
Create stability from chaos.
The eternal dance plays on
In nature and within us.

Blues Villanelle*

Don't tell me I can't sing the blues
Based solely on my house's site.
You can't see how I've paid my dues.

This may come as surprising news
But my path here has not been bright.
Don't tell me I can't sing the blues.

The painful steps I've had to choose
Are not apparent to your sight.
You can't see how I've paid my dues.

Head-on I promise you would lose
Should all our trials come to light.
Don't tell me I can't sing the blues

Until you've stood inside my shoes
And walked about until tonight
You can't see how I've paid my dues.

Knock my performance, if you choose
But beyond that, you have no right.
Don't tell me I can't sing the blues.
You can't see how I've paid my dues.

* A villanelle consists of five tercets and a quatrain that follow a
  specific 2-rhyme scheme that incorporates repeated phrases.

My Poem

My poem is loved
But she doesn't love me back.
She complains,
With beautiful brunette locks
As shiny as they could be,
That she'd rather be a blonde.

Flashbacks

It has been said that when you die
Your life passes before your eyes.
Occasionally while doing something mundane
Driving my car down a familiar road
Or waiting in line at the supermarket
Panic suddenly strikes.
I become paralyzed with fear
As the thought hits me:
I might be in my final moments
Watching the flashback.
There must be some way to save myself
From whatever situation I'm in
Rather than viewing this flashback.
No, there can't be any way out
Or I wouldn't be seeing this last-minute replay.
I'm not sure whether I'm living
Or using my final breath to observe my life
But I know one thing:
If this is my end,
I would rather spend it unaware.
I resolve to relax and concentrate
On making a good flashback for myself.

Dandy Lions

The least imaginative eye
can see their yellow manes.
Some see their stems dancing
with top hats and canes.

But their name is
Not dandy lions at all.
They are named
After lion's teeth.

This truth
Like so many others
Is hard to accept.

My Fair Ladies

Are there lilac trees in the heart of town?
    Blanche DuBois
    depended on the
    kindness of strangers.
Can you hear a lark in any other part of town?
    Norma Desmond
    posed for the camera.
It's just on the street where you live.
    Sylvia Plath actually lived.
    No lilacs.
    No larks.

The Camel

The heat rises
In waves off the sand
Across it, a camel moves
Oh so slowly
With huge strides
Sensuously
In the rhythm of the heat

Poet School

Do you think there's a school where poets go?
Somehow I don't think so.
Could you see Lord Tennyson
In Creative Writing 101?
Or imagine teaching rhyme schemes
To sweet, neurotic Emily?
Do you think a teacher would detect
Frost's subtleness and intellect?
And who on Earth would share a locker
With sloppy, brash Dorothy Parker?

* "Poet School" was previously published in *Elmhurst Imprints, Arts Beat,* and the *Aardvark Adventurer.* "Poet School" was awarded Honorable Mention in the Formal Verse category of Poet's and Patrons Awards.

Fun with Yoo

Want to go to the zoo, Sue?
We could view a few from Peru,
wear blue shoes and stand in a queue.
Or in lieu, bring Hugh, the Sioux
And maybe Lou too
To see a movie starring Winnie the Pooh
or Scooby Do.

Carried to Concerts

Carried to concerts before being born
This mama's child's soul was adorned
With bongos and bells and balmy rhyme
A heart that beats in calypso time

Love and music thus instilled
That joyful mind is always filled
With harmonic and melodic schemes
Vibrantly colored pieces of dreams

* "Carried to Concerts" was previously published in *Mobius: The Poetry Magazine*.

Music's Advantage

A poet writes "temptation"
but a musician melts
that first syllable
"Tem mmmm mmm"
for an agonizingly long time.
You can feel the "mmmm"
purred into your ear
dizzying your head
with what-ifs.
Then comes the "tay"
a quick pang of reality
before the key drops to
some visceral, guttural octave
causing a shiver through you
for the last "shun."

Destiny Revealed

That connection between
The bakery with upturned eaves
And my private life
Is created mystically.
Wearing nets,
Fishermen of fortune
Stir the potion,
Bake with dragon smoke,
Print and place the treasured writings.
East meets west as it's folded,
Carried to where it waits
Until some predetermined time
When the almond-eyed lady
Dressed in silk
Hands it to me
And it knows
My future.
My secrets.

At the Art Institute

Caillebotte's painting is huge!
At least seven feet tall
And even wider.

Many things are happening
But the memorable one
Is the white pearl earring.

You might not notice
There's a man with a ladder
Or one on a horse
Because you see the earring.

A shimmering pearl
Against her pale lobe
The woman ambles the street
Unaware of the glimmer.

The white pearl earring
Next to her dark, pinned hair
On a gloomy, grey-skyed day.

That little bead
Contrasts with the
Delicate, black veil on her face.

The white pearl earring
A solitary sparkle
In an array of cobblestones
And umbrellas.

Langston Hughes' Dream

I know what happens
To a dream deferred
It drives to work
Day after day
It buckles the seat belt
Stops for the train
It holds on to a railing
Safely stops at a light
I know what happens
But I don't know why

Like Flying

I love to jump rope.
Arms out to the side
Like wings of a hawk.
The sun bathes my body.
The spinning rope
Creates a breeze
Blowing back my hair.
Without thought
My legs move in time
Lightly touching the ground
Just enough to appease gravity.

Dream Car

When I was younger
I wanted to drive a Checker Marathon.
I imagined I would paint it shiny black
Like a fat, round limousine.

Maybe I would outfit it with
Top-of-the-line woofers and tweeters
To turn up loud on crazy nights
Or lower on playful days.

My friends could ride
On those pop-ups in the back.
We'd fill that big-enough-for-suitcases trunk
With picnic stuff and oooo-ooo blankets.
We would be the coolest
As we cruised through the drive-thru.

I could probably buy that dream car today
Except that now, the dream
Is more about being young enough to enjoy it.

A FEMALE PERSPECTIVE

Friends

We played Barbies
Hide and seek
We sat in your room
Talking, giggling
We practiced how ladies walk
Made ourselves up
We held each other
Through heartaches
Heartbreaks
We stood up for weddings
Celebrated childbirths
We laughed, cried, hugged
Mourned and rejoiced.
Closer than sisters
We are friends.

Dear Women

Why do we hide
What makes us who we are?
Pregnant idols
We hold the future.
Common nobility
We embody strength.
Why do so many of us
Cover what's real
With talk of china patterns
and backsplash tiles?

A Visible Sign

In the drizzling rain
Kindred spirits with wounded hearts
Gathered in need of healing.

Out of that dreary day, a whiteness emerged
A sign of hope in the form of a bird.

With her head lifted and her wings spread
She glided over the water with such pride
That her gray and wrinkled reflection
Was invisible to all.

Her message was not lost.

Beach Boys Lyrics

We were young
Wind in our hair
We sang to each other
"God only knows
What I'd be
Without you"

Years have gone by
A foolish piece of me is gone.
I have grown, been successful
Had a good life.

Everyone
Knows what I am
Without you.

What Animal?

I don't know
what animal I'd like to be
but I know what I am.
I'm a bird who can't fly,
a lion without a roar,
a monkey who cooks and cleans,
aware of my own mortality.

Their First Kiss

It was a time removed
From time's normal rhythm,
The ebb and flow of days and nights
Occurring in a moment.
The spring of the year
Melting a wintry past
And with it many fears.
The kiss breathed a genesis
A penetrating warmth
Awakening each layer in its turn
To a gentle cascade of passion.

Pockets

If only my skirt had pockets
And I had something
To fill them
Pockets full of dreams
Oleander
Little purple blooms
Wafting all around me
Lifting me up
To where pockets wouldn't matter

This Fish

Watching fish can be calming.
But not this fish.
This fish knows she's trapped in a bowl.
She knows that if she doesn't eat
Everything that's fed to her
Her gills will be choked.
This fish knows that she has no voice;
Her life is totally dependent
On someone much bigger.
No, this fish cannot help me.

Deliciously Distracted

This morning as I loaded the dishwasher
The sound of the Nevilles came over the radio.
The robe I wore was reflected in the oven door.
Its hem moving to the music across the floor.

I could feel a warm breeze touching my face.
And a pulsating slinkiness took over the place.
In a moment the entire kitchen was gone
My robe transformed to a silky sarong.

My body could feel the sun's healing heat
As I danced unabashedly near a placid palm tree.
The scent of jambalaya wafted through the air.
Thank you, Mr. DJ for bringing me there.

*   "Deliciously Distracted" was previously published in *Arts Beat*.

The Drive-Thru

Two happy youths
Pulled into the drive-thru.
He ordered career success,
A good sex life,
And plenty of belly laughs.
I ordered nothing but
Happiness for him.
Bags in hand,
Miles down the road, I realize
It's too late to change my order.

* "The Drive Thru" was previously published in *Arts Beat*.

The Dream

Making her way to the timeclock
Today down a cruel city block,
Through icy November gales,
It's the dream, not the wind, that prevails.
The dream is of a magical man
With a surfboard strapped atop his van
Who in fanciful colors in the carefree sun
Had hair-flipped his way into her imagination.

Penis Envy

The burden of monthly cycles
And the uneven
Division of reproduction
Are annoying.
But to be envious
Of his parts
Would be like a living creature
Being jealous
Of a pull-toy's string.

I Don't Get It

What's with those wives
who stand by their husbands
no matter what kind of
announcement they make?
I'm waiting to see a wife
who would behave as I would.
If my husband said
he was stepping down
because he had an affair
or did something disgusting,
I would walk with him
arm-in-arm to the podium
wait until all of the cameras
were on him,
shout, "You pig!"
and slap him in the face
for all the world to see.

My Purse

My purse has two compartments.
They hold everything I need.

One side has my credit cards,
Cash, checks, and ID.
For this consumer society
It's everything I need.

The other side holds my make-up,
A variety of paint
For any mood I choose to feign.

Everything I need
To cover up my blemishes,
To hide my imperfections
So others cannot see.

There's also a mirror
Which comes in handy
When I look into my eyes
And tell myself
It's everything I need.

Letters

I love them.
Those funny little squiggles I learned to make on paper.
In childhood I discovered how each represents a sound,
Combinations make words or thoughts.
I enjoyed that game
The excitement of having words
Recognized by another.

In my mind's eye I see your silhouette
Your outward movements
As you open the envelope; unfold the note,
Your feelings as each sentence is revealed.

I still experience the joy
Of expressing myself in ink
But it's no longer a game.
It's the part of me that will live on
To love and caress you
Long after I'm gone.

His Grammar

I don't know
how she could fall
for a man whose
grammar is all wrong.

When he writes her letters
he says, "i Love you"
with the L in love
capitalized
but "i" is lower case,
the same as "you."
Then
he writes "eachother"
like it's one word.

On second thought,
Maybe I do understand.

---

* "His Grammar" was originally published without a title in *The Sun.* It was the caption for a photograph of me writing in my backyard. This poem earned an Honorable Mention in the Poets and Patrons Awards.

Dating 101

A bear is secure, comfortable
Lions, strong and proud
Puppies are friendly
Avoid the wolf
And you'll be alright

Because He Used Film

I stood at the photo counter
anxious to see the vacation shots
my husband took
of me in my swimsuit.
I was looking pretty good.
I remember how proud I was
as I smiled for those pictures.
Finally, at long last
tear open the envelope.
Oh no!
It seems he cut off my head
but got a perfectly focused shot
zoomed in on my cleavage!
If he had used the digital camera
I could have clobbered him
right there on the spot.

Seen from an Outdoor Café

He on his side of the street
And she on hers
Each yelling obscenities
And answering like mirrors.
Her friends tried to hold her back
While his attempted with him.
It's easier to understand
When you know
They were equally passionate lovers.

Unfinished Business

She came home one day
To find the back door blocked
By a huge wooden panel.
When she asked her husband
What is was there for,
He said it was there for "a while."
And he was right.
   Apparently, he was going
   To fix the porch with it.
   But he never finished.

Then one day, she came home
And every room in the house
Had holes cut into the ceiling.
When she asked her husband
What he was doing,
He said, "nothing right now."
And he was right.
   Apparently, his plan was
   To put in central air.
   But he never finished.

One day she came home
A bit early from work
To find him
With another woman.
   He didn't finish that either!

Brown Eyes

When your strong arms are holding me
And your chest's against my cheek
I melt into your fragrance
And listen to your heart beat
I can feel my troubles fading
As I lift my gaze to meet
Your adorable brown eyes
Always comforting to me

The Wedded Trees

A pair of married trees stood in our backyard
One was a maple, the other an ash.
They grew over and through each other.
In the winter, their limbs were braided
In a lacy pattern against the sky.
In the spring, a peek would reveal
Their beautiful, subtle differences.
Yet, when summertime came,
You might be convinced
That you were seeing one tree.
They played out their married routine
Through every season.
In the fall of each year
The two revealed their separate personalities.
The ash became a brilliant yellow
While the maple sported orange and red.
The festivity of autumn between them
Was a sight to behold.
Each passing year these wedded trees
Performed their dance
Melding together and showing their own strengths.

When one grew sick
It seriously threatened
The health of the other
Supporting the hollowing limbs.

A few years later, the lone spouse looks well
The hole in the ground has been covered
But there will always be
A hole in the sky.

Breathless

I feel more beautiful this morning
Than the sonnets heard last night.
With the morning sun
Comes memories of candlelight,
A dance without music,
A kiss in the dark,
And you, like the poet's words
Immortalized within my heart.

* "Breathless" was previously published in the Valentine's Day
  issue of *Chime Magazine*.

Peaches

I remember the peaches we bought that day
And how we shared them
Juice running down our forearms
And faces.

I remember how we laughed
And playfully licked the sweet drops
From each other.

That was the first time I ever really tasted peaches.

Tonight

Mostly it's this quiet time,
In my pajamas,
That I think of you.
After the evening news
You would lighten the mood
With a joke or two.

I didn't always understand
But you never explained.
It made your meaning
Even funnier
When it hit me later.

You were the first gray-haired man
I ever thought was attractive.
I laugh each time I think about
When you put on that silly hat
Saying, "Sis Boom Bah"
Was the sound of a sheep exploding.

Many dreamed of sitting next to you,
I was content just to see you.
I thought you and your calming voice
Would always be there.

I was young then.
And not much older when you,
Your clubless swing,
And your Bill Blass suits,
Went away.

I miss you Johnny.

The Chess Game

Ebony captured Snow's bishop
Unwittingly leaving his own queen at risk

While the men played chess
Ebony's wife gathered flowers in the garden
She carefully chose each bloom
Touched each to her tender cheek
Sensuously sampling its delicate perfume

Snow's eyes quickly returned to the chessboard
With thoughts of taking the queen

As If

Sometimes, all these years later,
The sound of the rain
Or the sweet taste of cola
Can make me cry.

Not because I remember
All those times when
We were teens
Parked in our place
Across from McDonald's
To watch a storm.

But because I recall one night
Months after we broke up
I went on a rainy night
First date.

When we parked in that same place,
He told me that you
Had shared the secret with him.

As if the rain
And this place
Were all we ever were.

The Broken Ring

She bandaged her ring with adhesive tape
Where the setting's broken, it starts to chafe.
Yet on one knee that fateful night
My God, it really felt so right.

It's been fixed so many times before
The tiresome ritual's became a bore.
That faulty spot never adheres
Even after all these years.

They have two kids and took a vow.
She adds more tape and prays somehow
That it stays in place, at least for now.

The Alpha Man

He is a gorilla
Pounding his chest
Or brushing his teeth

He's a grizzly bear
With thick, heavy limbs
Raking the leaves

He is a fierce lion
Protecting his pride
Or rolling with his mate

Awakening

There's a mystical connection like the moon and the tide
Between that place in my heart and my watery eyes
That place you reached with your words
Your words I recognized as once being my own
> Long ago
> Before my heart was abandoned
> To collect dust
Dust that would have turned to stone
If not for your words to remind me
> I cannot live without love

* "Awakening" was previously published in *Elmhurst Imprints Magazine*.

CONSEQUENCES OF BIRTH

Music of Family

The music has gone through many phases
From tunes about sunshine and patty cake
To ditties about reptilian ninjas,
Or whatever was on the radio.

Some songs always stay the same:
An ancient refrain my mother sang sweetly
As she rocked me off to sleep;
The spirituals born of hardship,
Ballads that made my grandpa cry.

No matter what shape the melody takes
The power within it remains the same.

A mother's voice whispers in the highest tree branch
And weaves into the earth like the roots of the grass.
As the rain that quietly hushes,
It urges us to "hold strong ... hold strong."
And like the thunder when it crashes,
It shouts for us to stand against the storm.

Stand against the storm!

* "Music of Family" is the only poem I've ever written for
performance purposes. It was performed at Fermilab
Arts Series Poetry Slam and was previously published in
Bellowing Ark.

Dealing a Refuge

Our family patriarch
Surrounded by teams of doctors and nurses
We wait in the next room

A wedge of cards fits into my hand
Its edges comfortable and smooth
The purr of the shuffle
Brings muffled images of
Childhood Kings and Queens
The laughter, the grown-ups talking
Bid, and meld, and trump
Would lull me into sleep

Like solitary steps down a path
The cards click into place
One up six down, one up five down
The familiar triangle emerges
With soothing predictability

Black on red, red on black,
Counting backwards in an ether-like trance
Broken only by the appearance
Of the Queen without a King

Just a Swoosh

All I heard
Was just a "swoosh"
Over the sound of the vacuum.
I kept cleaning the car
Parked in the driveway
Next to the pool.
I was aware of no other sound.
That's when the explosion
Of quiet hit me.
I felt the concussion in my chest.
Thank God, I heard the silence in time.

I Saw a House

it was a beautiful house
such that i
could never have

victorian, yellow
manicured lawn with tulips
a fine wooden table
a reflected chandelier

how nice it would
be to dine at such
a table with matched dishes
heavy silver
kitchen cabinets
filled to the ceiling

and in the bath
to wrap myself
in thick warm towels
wiggling toes into
a soft comfy carpet

that's when i saw it

emotions of
tears welled in my eyes

that familiar blue star
in the window

carpets don't matter
when children are not safe

i cried for parents
i cried
for my own shallowness
and for the foolishness
of all mankind

Sedentary Lifestyle

After retiring from the railroad
Much to his doctor's dismay
Grandpa led a sedentary life.
He spent his days
Reading with glasses perched on his nose,
Listening to music from records, and
Watching quiz and travel shows on TV.
He would entertain us
With wonderfully imaginative stories.
He was sedentary
The way a book is sedentary.
From his chair, he went places
No jogger could reach.
He taught us to see
Beyond what is visible.

Zoom

Handlebars slice through the sunny day
"Hey, watch how fast I can go!"
Hair blown back like Mercury's wings,
Little leg muscles
Move pedals up and down
With piston speed.
His face turns pink
His smile gleams.
That was only the beginning
Of how fast it all would go.

For My Little Daughter

When I first saw you
I didn't know you would have such curly hair
I didn't know you would be such a good girl
So pretty
I didn't know you would have such nice white teeth
And smile so beautifully
But I hoped it
I hoped it all

The Chair

I'm sorry to see it go
But we got our money's worth.
There it was at the shopping mall closing,
A grotesquely ornate, extra-wide chair.

The auctioneer looked around
"Do I hear a dollar?"
"C'mon, just one dollar"
I raised my hand "Sold!"

Its curly wooden arms and lumpy red upholstery
Never fit our décor
But my children grew up with the magic
Of having Santa's chair in their playroom.

Come with Me

(A St. Patrick's Day Poem for My Mexican Friends)

I'll tell you a story
Of a young man
Alive but hungry
Who attended his own wake

He said goodbye to everyone he loved
Never to see them again
He kissed the girls and his mother
Shook hands with all the townsmen
And the next day
From the deck of a ship
He watched his beloved country
Glide away

I never met that man
Whose blood flows through my veins
He is in my blue eyes
My tenor voice
And I carry a piece of his broken heart

Come with me mis amigos mexicanos
To watch a parade
To toast a river dyed green
And to celebrate
Our shared immigrant experience

My Boy-Child

He sits quietly
Playing with toys
Calculating
Learning
Perfecting skills

He is suntanned
Beautiful
A product of
My own genes

He deserves better

Suburban Spoon Song

I put you in your highchair
Bowl in my left hand
Spoon in the right

Then our story tells us
Of a plate that ran off
With a spoon one night

We watch the movie-nanny
Make magic
With spoons and kites

Then Daddy and Mommy
Spoon through the night

Watermelon

Red and juicy
He calls it apple.
Delicate two-year-old
Fingers pick up
The bite-sized pieces
As I open the day's mail
And straighten the kitchen.
"Apple, apple" he cries
So I cut more
Watermelon.
The process repeats
Several times before I notice
His hands and arms
Drippy and sticky
Curls wet, matted to his forehead
Left eyebrow hairs locked upright
Little pink melon pieces
On one ear
And both knees!
His face bears
A huge smile
In the familiar shape
Of a watermelon wedge.

Birth of a Daughter

An image of a flower came from toil and pain.
A flower bloomed at the tip of a branch
Which itself had arisen from the tip of another.
I moved down into the bloom
Past branch after branch
Toward the trunk and the roots.

I returned to reality
Forever changed
My crucial life
Had become a link in a much greater chain.

I saw the world outside,
The sun, the rain
And all the rest,
The noise, the light,
Even the toil and the pain
As merely a distraction
From the truth
From the tree.

Mom

I don't want your dresser
Or your jewelry.
The memories are all I need:
An old house with
A rickety porch and a swing
Paintbrushes and pancakes
Hopscotch and hats.
I should apologize for the fights.
I am sorry.
Growing up was hard for me.

Fourteen Years

My son is fourteen now.
No one could understand
How he's changed my life,
The experiences we've had
And things we've been through.

But whenever I see a mom
With a specially-challenged child,
It takes all my strength
To stop myself from hugging her
And sobbing from the depths to the sky
"My baby too!"

* "Fourteen Years" was previously published in the United Kingdom, *Splizz Magazine*.

My Life is a River

The water in this section of the river flows
From mill to mill, working hard as it goes
But I find solace knowing that down the way
There's a quiet spot where children play

Coffee

This isn't very good coffee.
Childhood Sunday mornings
the smell was wonderful.
Occasional afternoons
Mom and the red lipstick ladies
pearls and smiles
red marks left on cups;
until one day
it was me and my friends
talking of movies and men.
Coffee always coffee.
And now
this bitter cup.
The cookies won't help
as one-by-one I'm greeted
by red lipstick ladies
with silver hair and teary eyes.

Adolescence

Of course I know myself.
I mean, we've never been formally introduced
Or anything like that
But who do you think I talk to when I sit
On the dresser and look in the mirror,
Or sing into my hairbrush to?

Of course I know myself.
What a dumb question.
How absurd to think I don't know who I am.
I'm the one who talks me out of things
Or sometimes into them.

Eternity

These acres were once buried
Under the weight of mile-thick glacial ice.
For millennia animals performed
Their dance of life and death right here.
There may have been a forest.
A native woman might have given birth
Right on this very spot.
But it also happens to be the site
Of my long-gone childhood home.
So, as I park my car
In this strip mall lot
I'm somewhere else.
For in my mind
That house stands for all eternity.

Her Hands

Nothing unusual
An ordinary cashier
I watched her hands on the register
Her hands became your hands
I couldn't take my eyes off them
I watched her hands, your hands
I wanted to touch them
To pull them toward me
I remembered the last time
They were cold
I didn't cry
Until I got home

* "Her Hands" was previously published in *The Prairie Light Review*.

Waiting by Your Bed

Myocardial infarction
Sounds like a funny word.

I think it's the "farc" part.

I hope some day
You and I will
Sit together
And laugh about
The funny "farc" word.

Chocolate Chip Cookies

There was a bakery
next to the roller rink.
Some people walked
with skates hung
over shoulders.
Others drove
in convertibles.

An ever-present
radio played
and when the magic
was just so

the whole neighborhood
was bathed
in the scent
of chocolate chip cookies.

The Hub*

There it was
Past the jukebox
And the popcorn
A huge expanse
Of oval-shaped, shiny, wooden floor.

The place where you could sail out
Feel the wind in your hair
Lean into the curve,
And hear that
Undeniable, irreplaceable
Purr of tiny wheels
Gliding over hardwood planks.

* The Hub was a roller rink on North Harlem Ave. in Chicago
  (Norridge), Illinois.

The Photo Album

I remember the day that photo was taken.
No one ever says, "Let's record
how foolish we are."
But somehow that's all we see.

An Eye Opener

Arm raised over his head
Tumbling off the sofa toward the floor
Exposed nipples, taut flesh
His photo hangs
On my daughter's bedroom wall.
Shocked by his near-naked image
But even more by the fact
That my baby girl is growing up.

Washing Dishes

When I was eleven,
and had to wash dishes by hand;
they were my archenemy.
Dishes chained me to the sink
in the fruity-wallpapered kitchen
as summer breezes
brought the scent of jasmine
and freedom
through the window.
My hands in soapy water while
fireflies, unaware of my plight,
danced happily in the yard.
I wanted to escape that awful place.

Then today, a broken dishwasher
brought me once again
face-to-face with my
lifelong nemesis. This time
revealed a surprising twist.
With hands in soapy water,
I can feel a long-ago breeze,
recall the smell of jasmine,
imagine little yellow sparkles in
the grass, and blissfully
remember my mother's kitchen.

As the Big Hand Clicks

Some go to Times Square
Others fill the bars
Tonight my aunt's house
Will be crowded
With people and with memories

We will find comfort
In our illusion of control
As the big hand clicks
From East to West

Then as this year
Becomes last year
We will cling to each other
As once more
We are hurled around the sun

* "As the Big Hand Clicks" was previously published in *The Kane County Chronicle.*

ALPHABETICAL LIST OF POEMS

Alphabetical List